Cornwall and Slavery

Paul White

Bossiney Books • Exeter

The eminent abolitionist Olaudah Equiano,
whose autobiography and lecture tours were an inspiration to
the abolition movement

First published 2021 by
Bossiney Books Ltd, 68 Thorndale Courts, Whitycombe Way,
Exeter, EX4 2NY

www.bossineybooks.com

ISBN 978-1-906474-93-5

Printed in Great Britain by Booths Print, Penryn

Introduction

In the history of Cornwall, as in every other part of Britain, there were people who made their fortunes from plantations worked by enslaved Africans, and even from the slave trade itself.

Most people now accept that this needs to be acknowledged, though there are those who believe, or would like to believe, that the British Empire was from the beginning a scheme designed to bring progressive civilisation to the world, emulating the supposed wonders of the Roman Empire, rather than, at least to start with, a highly successful commercial enterprise by which our businesses brought wealth to Britain, and in which, for a long time, with naval support and latterly with much broader government involvement, we proved better than our European rivals at exploiting the world. And its peoples.

The history of slavery makes uncomfortable reading, but it is best that we face the realities of the past. And those realities include questions as to why it roused so little opposition for so long – not to find excuses, but to understand how people in the past thought and reacted. Explanation is not justification.

However, there is more than that to the story of Cornwall's connections with slavery. My initial research for this book was inspired by the life stories of two men from very different backgrounds, Thomas Pellow of Falmouth who was captured by Barbary pirates and enslaved in Morocco for 23 years before escaping and writing his autobiography, and Joseph Emidy from Guinea, enslaved in Brazil, who became leader of the Truro Philharmonic Orchestra.

I wanted to know more about the historical context of these lives, and I can only hope that readers will find the background as interesting as I did.

Paul White

Slavery in the ancient world

In Ancient Rome and its empire, which for a time included Cornwall at its very periphery, slavery was normal – as it had been in Egypt, Greece and elsewhere for millennia. The senators and other aristocrats of Rome demonstrated their wealth and importance by their huge households, consisting mostly of slaves, to such an extent that slaves in Rome quite possibly outnumbered free citizens. These slaves included soldiers and influential bureaucrats as well as servants and labourers.

Where did the slaves come from? The main source was warfare: when a large battle occurred between rival states, the warriors on the losing side were all on some occasions slaughtered, but more often they were taken prisoner: the rich among them would be ransomed, but most would be sold in slave markets.

However, warfare in those days, and well into the Middle Ages, was very often about looting: and the loot included people. Most slaves were victims not of great battles but of border raiding, and women and children were valued as well as men. There were long-distance slave trading routes, many of which led to Rome.

There is a story that Pope Gregory I, visiting a slave market around AD 590, saw some pale-skinned boys with blue eyes and, being told that they were Angles, joked *'Non Angli sed angeli, si forent Christiani.'* ('Not English but angels, if only they were Christians.') This is said to be the moment when he decided to send Augustine to Britain to convert its people.

Perhaps Gregory fancied purchasing some boys for his household: certainly there is no suggestion that he regarded slavery as wrong – and neither the Catholic church nor its later Protestant rivals seem to have done so, though there were individuals such as Bishop Wulfstan, who in AD 1008 drew up laws prohibiting the export of Christian slaves from England. (Non-Christian slaves were excluded from this law.)

After the Roman armies left Britain around AD 400 – and quite possibly before – British coasts were being raided for slaves.

4

The boys Gregory saw had been taken from the kingdom of Deira (approximately the East Riding of Yorkshire). On the western side of Britain, St Patrick was captured by Irish raiders but it is not known from where exactly: Cumbria is likely, Scotland or Wales possible – maybe even Cornwall. The date also is unknown but it was probably fairly early in the 5th century. Patrick remained a slave for six years before escaping.

By the 8th century those enterprising characters the Vikings had established trading posts in Ireland, notably at Dublin, and were sending trading missions to Britain to purchase slaves. They probably had a number of contact points in Britain, but are known to have dealt with a market at Bristol, where presumably the local Anglo-Saxon merchants purchased slaves taken in warfare and raiding so that they could sell them to the Viking traders, whose networks stretched from Russia to the Mediterranean.

Domesday Book

A rather different form of slavery co-existed with the trade in slaves, and is evident in Domesday Book. Across the whole area it covered – most of England and some parts of Wales – *servi* (Latin for slaves) represent about 10% of the population of agricultural workers, but the further West, the larger the proportion. In Cornwall the figure is a massive 1111 *servi*, nearly 22% of the workers enumerated. Probably the figures include only adult males, not their wives and children. The survey did not cover all inhabitants: landowners, servants and soldiers in the castles and monks in monasteries are none of them included, nor are townsfolk. Bodmin was said to contain 68 houses, but there are no figures for the other towns.

It has been a matter of scholarly contention whether *servus* in Domesday Book should be translated as 'slave' or 'serf'. I am going to use serf, in order to distinguish it from slavery as we usually understand it.

It is uncertain quite what the status of a Domesday Book serf was, and whether it was the same across the whole of England, but it seems likely that most Cornish serfs were allotted a small piece of land to grow their own food, and if they were both careful and lucky they might even make some income for themselves, in a few cases sufficient to buy their freedom.

[Our word 'slave' comes from the Byzantine Greek for Slav: by the 9th century Slavs formed a large element of the slaves both in the Eastern Empire and in the Mediterranean Muslim world.]

The serfs were owned by the landowner, but if ownership of the land changed, they automatically became the property of the new owner. The owner could not take them to the local market and sell them, and he was responsible for their housing and feeding. There is a huge contrast between being tied for life to the village where you were born (bad enough) and being conveyed in shackles to another continent, sold in a market to the highest bidder and forced to work in dire conditions on a plantation. Serfdom was a lesser evil than slavery.

It was possible for serfs – later called bondsmen – to gain their freedom, and that of their family, by 'manumission'. This could be either by a payment to their owner, or through the owner's generosity – whether out of kindness or piety.

There is a remarkable document listing Bodmin manumissions between AD 938 and 1100, bound into a book of the gospels. Of the 129 serfs freed, most had Cornish names, whilst two thirds of their owners had English names. This used to be thought evidence of Saxons having enslaved Cornish people, but it is now known that the number of Anglo-Saxon immigrants into England as a whole was far fewer than used to be assumed. The Anglo-Saxon takeover was less a matter of people-replacement and genetics than of cultural change. In such circumstances, the wealthier members of society tend to adapt faster to new economic conditions; they accept the new language as a tool of power and themselves often take new names.

It is generally suggested in popular history books that serfdom ceased to exist as a result of the Black Death, when the peasants acquired economic power as their numbers declined, and land-owners were desperate for labour. There is some truth to this. The growth in towns also made it easier for a serf to run away: if he remained at liberty for a year, he was automatically free.

However, serfdom had not ended. In 1574 Queen Elizabeth's government set up a commission to identify the remaining bondsmen and bondswomen in Cornwall, Devon, Somerset and Gloucestershire, and what property each held. They would then be offered their freedom – at a price. For Elizabeth's Treasury, this was potentially a good source of income at a time when the Crown was strapped for cash, whilst the economy was booming. It is not clear how many of her grateful serfs responded.

The Barbary pirates

Slave raiding had not ceased. The crusades, and subsequent wars between Muslims and Christians, made the Mediterranean an area of competition, each side making slaves of the other as best they could. The most famous captive was perhaps Miguel de Cervantes, author of *Don Quixote*, who was captured in 1575 and remained a slave for five years until ransomed by friars.

This chaotic situation in the Mediterranean gave impetus to merchants, those of Spain and Portugal in particular, to look for new markets, and encouraged them to invest in exploration, most famously Christopher Columbus 'discovering' America, and Vasco da Gama rounding the Cape of Good Hope. And those voyages in turn led both to trade with Africa and to the colonisation of the Atlantic Islands – Madeira, the Azores, Cape Verde, where the Portuguese used African slaves to cultivate sugar, and the Canary Islands. The Spanish began to colonise South America. Here was the beginning of the slave trade as we know it.

But a quite different trade began around the same time. The Muslims of North Africa were not content with raiding within the Mediterranean to supply the Arab slave markets. They began to raid along the Atlantic coast, and even as far North as Scotland. The Western coast of Britain was very vulnerable, and especially Cornwall. The 'Barbary pirates' initially concentrated on shipping – a Government report in 1625 said 'The Turks are upon our coasts. They take ships only to take the men to make slaves of them.'

But they also attacked coastal settlements, taking 60 men, women and children in Mount's Bay in 1625, and repeatedly attacking St Keverne. In 1645 another raid took 240 captives on the Cornish coast. The English Navy was all but non-existent at this point, arguably due to Stuart incompetence, and the coastal villages were defenceless. Fishing communities were terrified.

By 1640 there were 3000-5000 English people captive in Algiers alone, all hoping to be ransomed. But if they were not, they faced a horrific future as slaves.

On 8 February 1661 Samuel Pepys wrote in his diary:

> At noon to the Exchange… Here I met many sea commanders… and I went to the Fleece tavern to drink, and there we spent till 4 o'clock telling stories of Algier and the manner of life of slaves there; and truly, Captain Mootham and Mr Dawes (who have both been slaves there) did make me full acquainted with their condition there. As to how they ate nothing but bread and water. At their redemption, they pay so much for the water that they drink at the public fountains during their being slaves. How they are beat upon the soles of the feet and bellies at the liberty of their Padron… How the poorest men do use their slaves best. How some rogues do live well if they endent to bring their masters in so much a week by their industry or theft; and then they are put to no other work at all. And theft is there counted no great crime at all.
>
> Thence to Mr Rawlinson's, having met my old friend Dick Scobell, and there I drank a great deal with him; and so home and to bed betimes, my head aching.

Thomas Pellow

A much fuller account was given by Cornishman Thomas Pellow, in *The History of the long Captivity and Adventures of Thomas Pellow in South Barbary*. Voyages and travels were a popular literary genre, and Pellow may have invented or exaggerated some details, but in the main his narrative is accepted as true.

Pellow was a scholboy in Penryn, but at the age of 10 in 1715 was so bored learning Latin that his parents allowed him to take a voyage with his uncle, carrying pilchards to Genoa. On their return, their ship and two others were captured by pirates off Cape Finisterre. They were taken to Salé, a city near Rabat in Morocco, and Pellow was given to a favourite among the 4000 wives of Sultan Moulay Ismail Ben Sharif, schooled in Arabic and later given to her eight-year-old son.

When Pellow refused to convert to Islam, he was imprisoned in chains, beaten daily with 'a bull's pizzle', and fed bread and water. He was finally forced to convert, by torture of burning. He became a door-keeper of the harem, then was given a horse, served the Sultan himself, and married a relative of the Sultan. An embassy came and bought freedom for the majority of the English prisoners, but Pellow was by then an elite slave, the Sultan's servant, so not eligible. He became a soldier, and was put in charge of a significant number of (slave) troops.

Morocco was not a peaceful place. Pellow helped quell a rebellion, which involved killing the garrisons and civilians in several towns. At one point he writes:

> The execution of these three captives was performed by the hands of an Exeter man, whose surname I have forgot, though I very well remember his Christian one was Absalom, and that he often told me he was by trade a butcher.... And so ended this long and bloody rebellion, which took us up about seventeen months, and with loss on our side of fifteen thousand of our men.

After the Sultan's death, there was a further civil war. One of the soldiers under Pellow's command was a Devonshire man, William Hussey, another William Johnston, from Kent. Hussey and Pellow were keen to join an escape by stealing a sloop, but Johnston was not. So Pellow slashed Johnston in the face with his sword – then pretended, abetted by Hussey, that it was Johnston who was trying to steal the sloop and escape. The judge accepted a 40 ducat bribe from Pellow to pardon Johnston.

Thomas Pellow was a survivor. Most of those taken prisoner, unless ransomed, died in prison, or were made slave labourers or oarsmen in galleys if men, concubines or servants if women. A recent estimate is that more than a million Christians were enslaved in North Africa. Life was nasty, brutish and short. Pellow could perhaps consider himself lucky: he had an adventurous life, finally escaping and returning to Britain after 23 years of horrendous danger. But he seems to have accommodated himself to the brutal local culture. It is not an edifying story!

He had some problems being accepted back, and in Gibraltar was mistaken for 'a Moor', but finally arrived in the Thames.

> Now I went ashore at Deptford, and going directly to church, returned public thanks to God for my safe arrival in Old England, and received the charity of the minister and parish clerk, staying in the town eight days longer, during which I was civilly entertained by Mr William James, a Cornishman, Captain Peacock's steward; and amongst all the vessels bound down the river, finding none bound for Falmouth, I asked my friend Mr James what course I had best to steer. He told me my most likely way to get a passage would be for me to go to Beel's Wharf, a little below London Bridge on the Southwark side of the river, and there I might find one or more of the Cornish tin vesels, or some other bound for Plymouth.

In London he meets a nephew of the Moroccan ambassador,

whom he knows – and he seems more comfortable in his company than with English strangers. He is presented to the ambassador and finds he is in the newspapers – which say he is to be presented to the King – which is untrue. At last he gets a ship.

[We] got that day off Plymouth, and the next being Sunday, we got about four o'clock in the afternoon off Falmouth Pier; whence being to Penryn, the place of my nativity, no more than two miles, I got to the town in the evening.

And as my father's house was quite at the other end of the town – perhaps about half a mile – I was, before I could reach it, more than an hour; for notwithstanding it was almost quite dark, I was so crowded by the inhabitants that I could not pass through them without a good deal of difficulty – though this, I must own, was of a different and far more pleasing nature to me than my first entry into Mequinez, every one, instead of boxing me and pulling my hair, saluting me and, after a most courteous manner bidding me welcome home, being all very inquisitive with me if I knew them. Which, indeed, I did not, for I was so very young at my departure, and my captivity and the long interval of time had made so very great an alteration on both sides, that I did not know my own father and mother, nor they me; and had we happened to meet at any other place without being pre-advised, whereby there might be an expectation or natural instinct interposing, we should no doubt have passed each other, unless my great beard might have induced them to enquire further after me.

And now is the so long lost sheep again restored to his owners, after his long straying and grievous hardships amongst those monsters and ravenous wolves of infidelity, and safely returned to his parents, in the town of his nativity, being the 15th day of October 1738.

The triangular trade

The first British slave voyages of any significance were made by John Hawkins of Plymouth (1532-1595) whose father had previously traded with Africa for goods, rather than slaves. Hawkins' first voyage was in 1562, by which time an Atlantic slave trade already existed: Portugal and Spain had conveniently divided the southern continents between them, with the Pope's blessing. Spain had the Caribbean and most of South America, Portugal had Brazil and Africa. The consequence was that Portugal had a monopoly of supplying African slaves to the Spanish colonies, as well as to its own Brazilian sugar plantations.

Understandably, Protestant England did not like this cosy arrangement. Hawkins made three voyages to the Guinea coast in the 1560s, accompanied on the second and third by his young cousin Francis Drake, purchasing (or sometimes stealing from the Portuguese) Africans from there and taking them across to the Caribbean where Spanish plantation owners were happy to purchase them despite their government's ban on foreign merchants.

Hawkins attracted investment, including from Queen Elizabeth. For his third voyage he wrote to the Queen on 16 September 1567:

> The voyage I pretend is to lade Negroes in Genoya and sell them in the West Indies in troke [barter] of gold, pearls and emeralds whereof I doubt not but to bring home great abundance, to the contentation [sic] of your Highness...

The three voyages were of increasingly diminishing success, and the third indeed led to hostilities between England and Spain due to a Spanish deception at San Juan d'Ulloa. Hawkins subsequently devoted himself to rebuilding the Navy, which he did with great effect in time for it to meet the Armada. Drake in his mature years found privateering (licensed piracy) was much more profitable than the slave trade.

English involvement was limited over the next 100 years, until the real development of the 'triangular trade'. This consisted of selling quality goods to the West African states, then taking slaves to Brazil, the Caribbean or North America on the 'middle passage', and returning, not with gold and pearls, but with goods saleable in England – sugar, tobacco and cotton. From that point the trade expanded at great speed and together with slavery on the plantations became an enterprise on an industrial scale.

Whilst Cornish vessels were sometimes involved, neither Cornish nor Devon ports were central to this trade. They may well have continued to find privateering more profitable, but the Crown had also established a monopoly of the slave trade for the London-based Guinea Company and later the Royal African Company.

Another reason was that the triangular trade required the right kind of goods to sell in Africa (especially Chinese and Indian silks), ready access to a strong market for the incoming goods, and above all an abundance of capital to invest in each voyage. In the seventeenth century there were two winners, London and Bristol. In the eighteenth century Liverpool came to dominate.

It is well known that the middle passage was in itself a terrible experience for the transported slaves, 20% of whom died during the crossing in the seventeenth century, and perhaps 10% with slightly improved conditions in the eighteenth.

One Falmouth family is known to have been involved: their father was an Irish ship's doctor, their mother the daughter of a Falmouth merchant. Thomas Corker (1669-1700) was sent as an apprentice to the Royal African Company on the Guinea coast.

He soon became an agent for them there, and married a local princess. In the 1690s he traded (contrary to the Company's rules) directly with his brother Robert (1668-1731) in Falmouth. Thomas was sacked by the Royal African Company in 1700, returned to Falmouth and died there. His mixed race descendants became rulers of that part of the Guinea coast, and became significant slave traders in their own right.

Thomas' brother Robert Corker meanwhile went from strength to strength. He served five times as Mayor of Falmouth, became Receiver of the Duchy of Cornwall in 1708 and bought property in and around Bossiney in North Cornwall, where he became MP for the borough. Then things went wrong, and on his death at Westminster in 1731 he owed no less than £23,000 in arrears to the Duchy.

Both brothers brought female slaves back to Falmouth, and Robert Corker continued to trade in slaves after Thomas's death. In 1705 he presented his widowed mother with a teenage servant, who was baptised with her new name Elizabeth Chegoe at Falmouth in July 1705.

The slave owners

For the most part, slaves arriving in the Caribbean were sold to plantation owners there, but some were transferred to North America, especially Georgia, and others were brought back to Britain to become household servants. Some of the Caribbean plantation owners are known to have had Cornish connections; they may have been identified as slave owners from their wills, or other historic records, but it is hard to get a clear picture. Many names will be missing.

University College London has an online map of British addresses known to be associated with slavery (https://www.ucl.ac.uk/lbs), which helpfully also names individuals.

A major source of those names is the list of people compensated when slavery in British-controlled territories was abolished in 1833. The compensation amounted to a generous £20 million, at a time when an agricultural labourer might earn £25 in a whole year. Nothing went to the 800,000 enslaved people, of course, only to their owners.

One noticeable feature of the compensation list is that there are many times more Devon entries than Cornish – over twice as many, even after allowing for the relative size of the county populations. The reason is not that the Cornish were more sensitive to the ethics of slavery; rather that the seaside resorts of Devon (Torquay, Teignmouth, Dawlish, Exmouth and Sidmouth in particular) had in the pre-Victorian period developed as social centres, both in the holiday season and throughout the year. They had genteel meeting places, subscription libraries, balls and concerts. Many ex-colonials retired there, as well as gentlemen who would in the censuses be described as 'Independent', and ladies 'Living on own means'. They were living on income from shares or from family trusts, and probably took little interest in the ultimate source of their income, as long as it allowed them to continue living in the style to which they thought themselves entitled.

Nevertheless, there were some significant absentee plantation owners living in Cornwall, notably Sir Rose Price whose family had been in the Caribbean for generations. Between 1814 and his death in 1834 Price owned Trengwainton, and used his wealth to develop the gardens. He was compensated for 543 slaves. Sir John Molesworth of Pencarrow had inherited 3269 acres in Jamaica. George Cotsford Call of Landulph owned 276 slaves, William Mitchell, MP for Bodmin, owned 192, the Rev. William Sloane Wilson of Madron, born in Tobago, also owned 192. Quite a number of clergymen were owners.

And the enslaved

Unsurprisingly we know much less about them – they appear only in records kept by their owners, who had little interest in them apart from as property – but one outstanding voice is that of Olaudah Equiano a.k.a. Gustavus Vassa (c.1745-1797) who wrote an autobiography that became a best-seller. His *Interesting Narrative...* is available online, and the first volume in particular contains fascinating information, not only about his family background in the Igbo/Eboe region of Nigeria and his capture and enslavement (by other Africans) as a child (though some historians have questioned its accuracy) and his transfer to the West Indies, but about his experiences as a powder boy in the

Royal Navy, taking part in battles. Here are some extracts:

Thus I continued to travel, sometimes by land, sometimes by water, through different countries and various nations, till, at the end of six or seven months after I had been kidnapped, I arrived at the sea coast....

The first object which saluted my eyes when I arrived on the coast was the sea, and a slave ship, which was then riding at anchor, and waiting for its cargo. These filled me with astonishment, which was soon converted into terror when I was carried on board. I was immediately handled and tossed up to see if I were sound by some of the crew; and I was now persuaded that I had gotten into a world of bad spirits, and that they were going to kill me. Their complexions too, differing so much from ours, their long hair, and the language they spoke (which was very different from any I had ever heard) united to confirm me in this belief. Indeed such were the horrors of my views and fears at the moment, that, if ten thousand worlds had been my own, I would have freely parted with them all to have exchanged my condition with that of the meanest slave in my own country.

At last, when the ship we were in had got in all her cargo, they made ready with many fearful noises, and we were all put under deck, so that we could not see how they managed the vessel. But this disappointment was the least of my sorrow. The stench of the hold while we were on the coast was so intolerably loathsome, that it was dangerous to remain there for any time, and some of us had been permitted to stay on the deck for the fresh air; but now that the whole ship's cargo were confined together, it became absolutely pestilential. The closeness of the place, and the heat of the climate, added to the number in the ship, which was so crowded that each had scarcely room to turn himself, almost suffocated us.

This produced copious perspirations, so that the air soon became unfit for respiration, from a variety of loathsome smells, and brought on a sickness among the slaves, of which many died, thus falling victims to the improvident avarice, as I may call it, of their purchasers.

This wretched situation was again aggravated by the galling of the chains, now become insupportable; and the filth of the necessary tubs, into which the children often fell, and were almost suffocated. The shrieks of the women, and the groans of the dying, rendered the whole a scene of horror almost inconceivable. Happily perhaps for myself I was soon reduced so low here that it was thought necessary to keep me almost always on deck; and from my extreme youth I was not put in fetters. In this situation I expected every hour to share the fate of my companions, some of whom were almost daily brought upon deck at the point of death, which I began to hope would soon put an end to my miseries.

Often did I think many of the inhabitants of the deep much more happy than myself. I envied them the freedom they enjoyed, and as often wished I could change my condition for theirs. Every circumstance I met with served only to render my state more painful, and heighten my apprehensions, and my opinion of the cruelty of the whites. One day they had taken a number of fishes; and when they had killed and satisfied themselves with as many as they thought fit, to our astonishment who were on the deck, rather than give any of them to us to eat as we expected, they tossed the remaining fish into the sea again, although we begged and prayed for some as well as we could, but in vain; and some of my countrymen, being pressed by hunger, took an opportunity, when they thought no one saw them, of trying to get a little privately; but they were discovered, and the attempt procured them some very severe floggings.

One day, when we had a smooth sea and moderate wind, two of my wearied countrymen who were chained together (I was near them at the time), preferring death to such a life of misery, somehow made through the nettings and jumped into the sea: immediately another quite dejected fellow, who, on account of his illness, was suffered to be out of irons, also followed their example; and I believe many more would very soon have done the same if they had not been prevented by the ship's crew, who were instantly alarmed. Those of us that were the most active were in a moment put down under the deck, and there was such a noise and confusion amongst the people of the ship as I never heard before, to stop her, and get the boat out to go after the slaves. However two of the wretches were drowned, but they got the other, and afterwards flogged him unmercifully for thus attempting to prefer death to slavery.

In this manner we continued to undergo more hardships than I can now relate, hardships which are inseparable from this accursed trade. Many a time we were near suffocation from the want of fresh air, which we were often without for whole days together. This, and the stench of the necessary tubs, carried off many....

We did not know what to think of this; but as the vessel drew nearer we plainly saw the harbour, and other ships of different kinds and sizes; and we soon anchored amongst them off Bridge Town. Many merchants and planters now came on board, though it was in the evening. They put us in separate parcels, and examined us attentively. They also made us jump, and pointed to the land, signifying we were to go there. We thought by this we should be eaten by these ugly men, as they appeared to us; and, when soon after we were all put down under the deck again, there was much dread and trembling among us, and nothing but bitter cries to be heard all the night from these apprehensions, insomuch that at last the white people got some old slaves from the land to pacify us.

They told us we were not to be eaten, but to work, and were soon to go on land, where we should see many of our country people. This report eased us much; and sure enough, soon after we were landed, there came to us Africans of all languages. We were conducted immediately to the merchant's yard, where we were all pent up together like so many sheep in a fold, without regard to sex or age...

I stayed in this island for a few days; I believe it could not be above a fortnight; when I and some few more slaves, that were not saleable amongst the rest, from very much fretting, were shipped off in a sloop for North America. On the passage we were better treated than when we were coming from Africa, and we had plenty of rice and fat pork. We were landed up a river a good way from the sea, about Virginia county, where we saw few or none of our native Africans, and not one soul who could talk to me. I was a few weeks weeding grass, and gathering stones in a plantation; and at last all my companions were distributed different ways, and only myself was left. I was now exceedingly miserable, and thought myself worse off than any of the rest of my companions; for they could talk to each other, but I had no person to speak to that I could understand. In this state I was constantly grieving and pining, and wishing for death rather than any thing else.

While I was in this plantation the gentleman, to whom I suppose the estate belonged, being unwell, I was one day sent for to his dwelling house to fan him; when I came into the room where he was I was very much affrighted at some things I saw, and the more so as I had seen a black woman slave as I came through the house, who was cooking the dinner, and the poor creature was cruelly loaded with various kinds of iron machines; she had one particularly on her head, which locked her mouth so fast that she could scarcely speak; and could not eat nor drink. I was much astonished and shocked at this contrivance, which I afterwards learned was called the iron muzzle.

Soon after, I had a fan put into my hand, to fan the gentleman while he slept; and so I did indeed with great fear. While he was fast asleep I indulged myself a great deal in looking about the room, which to me appeared very fine and curious. The first object that engaged my attention was a watch which hung on the chimney, and was going. I was quite surprised at the noise it made, and was afraid it would tell the gentleman any thing I might do amiss: and when I immediately after observed a picture hanging in the room, which appeared constantly to look at me, I was still more affrighted, having never seen such things as these before. At one time I thought it was something relative to magic; and not seeing it move I thought it might be some way the whites had to keep their great men when they died, and offer them libation as we used to do to our friendly spirits....

One day the captain of a merchant ship, called the *Industrious Bee*, came on some business to my master's house. This gentleman, whose name was Michael Henry Pascal, was a lieutenant in the royal navy, but now commanded this trading ship, which was somewhere in the confines of the county many miles off. While he was at my master's house it happened that he saw me, and liked me so well that he made a purchase of me. I think I have often heard him say he gave thirty or forty pounds sterling for me; but I do not now remember which. However, he meant me for a present to some of his friends in England: and I was sent accordingly from the house of my then master, one Mr Campbell, to the place where the ship lay; I was conducted on horseback by an elderly black man (a mode of travelling which appeared very odd to me). When I arrived I was carried on board a fine large ship, loaded with tobacco, &c. and just ready to sail for England....

The ship had a very long passage; and on that account we had very short allowance of provisions. Towards the last we had only one pound and a half of bread per week, and about the same quantity of meat, and one quart of water a day. We spoke with only one vessel the whole time we were at sea, and but once we caught a few fishes. In our extremities the captain and people told me in jest they would kill and eat me; but I thought them in earnest, and was depressed beyond measure, expecting every moment to be my last...

However, all my alarms began to subside when we got sight of land; and at last the ship arrived at Falmouth, after a passage of thirteen weeks. Every heart on board seemed gladdened on our reaching the shore, and none more than mine. The captain immediately went on shore, and sent on board some fresh provisions, which we wanted very much: we made good use of them, and our famine was soon turned into feasting, almost without ending.

It was about the beginning of the spring 1757 when I arrived in England, and I was near twelve years of age at that time. I was very much struck with the buildings and the pavement of the streets in Falmouth; and, indeed, any object I saw filled me with new surprise.

One morning, when I got upon deck, I saw it covered all over with the snow that fell over-night: as I had never seen any thing of the kind before, I thought it was salt; so I immediately ran down to the mate and desired him, as well as I could, to come and see how somebody in the night had thrown salt all over the deck. He, knowing what it was, desired me to bring some of it down to him: accordingly I took up a handful of it, which I found very cold indeed; and when I brought it to him he desired me to taste it. I did so, and I was surprised beyond measure. I then asked him what it was; he told me it was snow: but I could not in anywise understand him.

He asked me if we had no such thing in my country; and I told him, No. I then asked him the use of it, and who made it; he told me a great man in the heavens, called God: but here again I was to all intents and purposes at a loss to understand him; and the more so, when a little after I saw the air filled with it, in a heavy shower, which fell down on the same day.

After this I went to church; and having never been at such a place before, I was again amazed at seeing and hearing the service. I asked all I could about it; and they gave me to understand it was worshipping God, who made us and all things. I was still at a great loss, and soon got into an endless field of inquiries, as well as I was able to speak and ask about things.

However, my little friend Dick used to be my best interpreter; for I could make free with him, and he always instructed me with pleasure: and from what I could understand by him of this God, and in seeing these white people did not sell one another, as we did, I was much pleased; and in this I thought they were much happier than we Africans. I was astonished at the wisdom of the white people in all things I saw; but was amazed at their not sacrificing, or making any offerings, and eating with unwashed hands, and touching the dead. I likewise could not help remarking the particular slenderness of their women, which I did not at first like; and I thought they were not so modest and shamefaced as the African women.

I had often seen my master and Dick employed in reading; and I had a great curiosity to talk to the books, as I thought they did; and so to learn how all things had a beginning: for that purpose I have often taken up a book, and have talked to it, and then put my ears to it, when alone, in hopes it would answer me; and I have been very much concerned when I found it remained silent.

My master lodged at the house of a gentleman in Falmouth, who had a fine little daughter about six or seven years of age, and she grew prodigiously fond of me; insomuch that we used to eat together, and had servants to wait on us. I was so much caressed by this family that it often reminded me of the treatment I had received from my little noble African master. After I had been here a few days, I was sent on board of the ship; but the child cried so much after me that nothing could pacify her till I was sent for again. ...

Equiano was clearly very astute, and despite many horrors and betrayals, by which he was returned to the West Indies, he finally managed to acquire enough money to purchase his own freedom. He became a hugely significant figure in the abolition campaign in England.

His book was written with a professionalism way beyond that of Thomas Pellow's, and was equally cleverly marketed.

Its very first reviewer – an unknown by the name of Mary Wollstonecraft – whilst generally impressed, thought that 'the narrative should have been closed when he once more became his own master.' She thought the second volume, including the 'long account of his religious sentiments and conversion to methodism' was 'rather tiresome'. It's a remark with which one can wholeheartedly agree!

Another freed slave who made a great impression in Cornwall was Joseph Emidy (c.1775-1835). Emidy was born in Guinea and was carried by Portuguese slave traders to work on Brazilian coffee plantations, but was later taken to Lisbon. There he was employed in the Portuguese royal court, where he was recognised for his appreciation of music. He was given a violin, and within four years held the position of second violin in the Lisbon Opera House, where he was particularly appreciated by the Cornish naval captain Sir Edward Pellew, who was waiting for his frigate the *Indefatigable* to be repaired.

Whether Emidy was at this point freed or still enslaved is unclear, but Pellew wouldn't have minded either way. Once the *Indefatigable* was ready to sail, he had Emidy kidnapped so that he could entertain the ship's crew, not with classical music but with jigs and hornpipes. It was only after four years, in 1799, that Emidy was given his freedom, even though slavery within Britain was by then not recognised by the law.

It was at that time very fashionable in Britain for the rich to have black servants or entertainers.

After 1799, Emidy flourished in Cornwall, as a music teacher, concert performer, and also organiser. He became leader of the Truro Philharmonic Orchestra, and is known to have composed concertos and piano music; sadly, none of his compositions have survived. He married Jenefer Hutchins in Falmouth in 1802, and they had eight children.

Another former slave/servant was Philip Scipio, whose gravestone in the church at Werrington, just north of Launceston, has the following inscription:

Deposited Here
Are the Remains of Philip Scipio
Servant to the Duke of Wharton
Afterwards to Sir William Morice
An African
Whose Quality might have done Honour
To any Nation or Climate
And Give Us to See
That Virtue is Confined

To no Country or Complexion
Here Weep
Uncorrupted Fidelity
And Plain Honesty
In pious regard to which virtue's approv'd…

Clearly there were cases where an enslaved servant became treasured by the family, particularly if like Philip he entered the household as a child, and died as a teenager.

Other forms of coercion and forced labour

Why was slavery accepted by Britain for so long, and why did it take so many years for it to be abolished? The Quakers famously took a leading part in the abolition movement, but one of Equiano's owners was a Quaker. Even the Friends had only started asking their colleagues to stop participating in the slave trade in 1758, and it took some decades more before the Quakers all agreed that slavery was immoral.

One reason for the apparent blindness, perhaps, was that there were so many other horrors which people saw around them. Public execution remained normal until 1868. The last execution of a woman by burning was as late as 1789. Hanging, drawing and quartering was used till 1803. Flogging was normal.

There were also practices not totally dissimilar to slavery. The first was **indentured labour**. An indenture was simply a written contract, but written contracts were not a norm of ordinary employment. The contract was for a number of years, often seven, and typically a desperate person in Britain or Ireland would sign up to work for a particular employer in an overseas territory without wages, but receiving food and lodging, in exchange for having the cost of their passage paid.

This system was in use from the early 17th century, preceding slavery in North America. In fact, once the Slavery Abolition Act had been passed in 1833, slaves in the West Indies were not freed, but forced into indentured labour. And the East India company used indentured labour in its tea plantations.

Indentured labourers had some rights, but not many. They could be sold to another employer without their consent, could not marry, and could be flogged. As with slave owners, some employers treated their servants far worse than others: many indentured labourers died prior to the end of their contract.

Transportation was even worse. It was seen as an alternative to execution, but could be applied for a very minor crime, such as poaching game, or the theft of any item worth more than a shilling (5p). The passage was often long and miserable. The prisoner could be in chains, food was minimal: as many as 20% did not survive the voyage to Australia. Once there, they were farmed out to settlers and treated much like slaves.

The press gang was a terror in every port. They simply captured men to serve in the Navy – in theory only experienced seamen were liable but, when desperate for crewmen, the press gang did not discriminate. A man could find himself effectively a prisoner on board a navy ship for years, and when finally released (probably only once a war ended) he might wait for years before being paid.

Under the system of **parish apprenticeships**, pauper children as young as seven were made 'apprentices' of local farmers or other businesses including factories. They could then be made to work hard in return for their keep, and be no charge on the parish. They might have no shoes or stockings: 'If we gave them shoes, they would run away,' was an explanation given to Poor Law Guardians.

My aim is to understand historic thought patterns. At the risk of seeming not to take slavery seriously, which I can assure you I do, perhaps I should also mention a bizarre analogy – **wife sales**.

The laws governing marriage were very strange by modern standards. On marriage, a husband took complete control of his wife's property and income, unless expensive legal arrangements had been made by her parents prior to the marriage in order to prevent this, and he also had such power over her that, when marriages were on the rocks, even among the upper classes it looked as though the husband owned the wife, although in law that was not the case. There was no Married Women As Property Act. But the legally ignorant behaved as though there was.

Everybody knew that divorce was impossible unless you could afford a special Act of Parliament. The solution some came up with was for the husband to take his wife to the local market and sell her to the highest bidder. A number of such incidents were reported in Cornish newspapers between 1810 and 1855. In most cases it is likely that the wife had agreed in advance to the procedure, and that her favoured new husband was the successful bidder. In 1818 the *West Briton* reported on an auction at Bodmin:

> A person called Sobey, who has lately been discharged from the 28th Regiment, bid sixpence for her and was immediately declared the purchaser. He led off his bargain in triumph, amidst the shouts of the crowd, and to the great apparent satisfaction of her late owner.

But it did not always work out completely to the satisfaction of the seller. At St Austell in 1835:

> On Friday last, the people assembled at St Austell market were surprised by the appearance of a man of advancing age leading a woman about thirty, by a halter which was tied round her waist.

Twopence was bid, then fourpence, which was accepted. Ex-wife and purchaser headed off to the pub to celebrate. But the husband had reckoned wthout the market official, who demanded that a market fee be paid. There being no agreed figure for the sale of a wife, they settled on the same fee as would have been paid for selling a pig.

It's crazy, but if people were thinking like that, how did they perceive *real* slavery, if they were aware of it at all?

Where did they draw a line between owning a pet dog or cat, owning the horse which they adored, and owning their own children? or their wife? Or their servant maid?

The abolition movement

In an English Common Law case in 1772 it was declared that slavery could not be enforced within England – but in practice enslaved people were subsequently forced to be indentured servants as long as they remained in Britain.

The use of British ships in the slave trade was made illegal in 1807. Conditions in the Caribbean had been expected to improve, but in fact they worsened. There were even more rebellions, and plantation owners and governments grew nervous.

Slavery in British colonies was made illegal in 1833.

Other countries gradually followed.

Confining the discussion to Britain, abolition was a great achievement, in the face of resistance. But that resistance was just as British as the abolition movement. Why was abolition so late and so slow?

As already suggested, conditions in Britain itself were grim to an extent that the horrors of slavery abroad didn't get much attention. And a large part of the answer may be that most people didn't even know about it, before there was a national press. They certainly had no way of knowing just how terrible the conditions were, until the abolition movement took off in the last decade of the 18th century, creating massive publicity through pamphlets and public meetings.

But perhaps even those people who *did* know, especially those who had power, did not see much wrong with it. After all, a classical education taught them that the ancient Greeks and Romans, who were their rôle models, had slaves. Just be nice to them, and it's OK to own slaves?

The Catholic Church and its successor the Church of England might occasionally object to the enslavement of Christians, but never of non-Christians. Plenty of churchmen appear in the compensation list: the Bishop of Exeter received £12,729 for 665 slaves. (The diocese of Exeter included Cornwall until 1876.) In the 18th century the established church was largely concerned with maintaining the *status quo*, one in which the Crown and the aristocracy were in full control, and this attitude was greatly reinforced after the French revolution, which could so easily have been replicated in Britain.

It was among the dissenters that abolitionism began – but in Parliament dissenters were seen by many as dangerous radicals who wished to destroy that *status quo*. An association with supposed revolutionaries cannot have helped the abolition cause. (Not all dissenters were abolitionists though: British Calvinists, in opposition to Arminian Methodists, actually *supported* slavery on the theological grounds that salvation did not depend on bodily freedom, and that calmly accepting suffering in this world was beneficial to the soul in the next.)

The first petition against slavery was presented to Parliament by Quakers in 1783. Methodists also played a large part, especially in Cornwall, where there were a number of anti-slavery societies. John Wesley instituted a boycott of sugar among Methodists, as a protest against slavery, and this was taken up in a big way. Putting sugar in your tea was just not acceptable in Cornwall – though apparently it was quietly accepted that sugar remained an essential ingredient to bake a pasty!

Undoubtedly a major factor was pervasive racism. Except among the Quakers, whose faith told them that all people were born equal, it was widely believed that all people were not equal.

Just as there was a social hierarchy in society, with Dukes inherently superior to dustmen, so it was throughout God's creation. There was a hierachy of animals, a hierarchy of plants, and of course therefore a hierarchy of races. White Europeans, especially Brits, were inherently superior to all others.

Many people in this period, even Wilberforce, also believed that Africans were so 'ignorant' that they were not yet ready for freedom. Wilberforce actually believed that until Africans had converted to Christianity (of his evangelical kind, no doubt) it was better for them to remain enslaved. Ending the slave trade was one thing, abolition of slavery quite another.

But the main driving force of resistance to abolition was the fact that those British colonies which were dependent on slavery, especially in the Caribbean, were huge producers of wealth. Britain's economy would suffer economic ruin, it was said, if slavery were abolished.

Perhaps those who consumed the sugar or the rum, wore cotton clothes or made a meagre living by working in cotton mills, would also have felt these were essentials for which slavery was an unfortunate necessity, but I suspect most were either totally unaware, or never thought about how those goods were produced, just as most of us today do not weigh up our responsibility for climate change at each and every shelf of the supermarket.

Whilst the number of British people directly involved in slave trading or plantation ownership was not great, very many more of 'the middling sort' were indirectly involved in colonial trade as merchants, investors, bankers, insurers or simply clerks. A surprising number of those compensated after abolition were not plantation owners, but wealthy people who had lent money on a mortgage basis to West Indian businesses – some of them even known to have been campaigners for abolition.

By the 1820s the mood was changing. More and more MPs, including Wynne Pendarves, elected for the County of Cornwall several times, were intent on reform of several kinds. Pendarves called for an enquiry into the 1819 Peterloo massacre (in which 18 people died when cavalry charged a Manchester crowd at a peaceful demonstration), parliamentary reform (Pendarves thought that enfranchising the middle class would eliminate the risk of revolution), a commutation of tithes and abolition of 'the monstrous evil' of slavery.

Lord Mount Edgcumbe, the Lord Lieutenant of Cornwall, regretted that 'a man of such pleasing manners in society and otherwise so respectable should have taken such an unfortunate line in politics'.

The abolitionist movement was in fact becoming increasingly

mainstream and respectable, with public meetings across Corn-wall, as elsewhere, sending petitions to Parliament demanding action. As its respectability grew, support for abolition among the political radicals actually diminished, because the cause was seen as a distraction from their more urgent concern – 'wage slavery' within Britain.

One of the most prominent radicals, a Devonian named Robert Carlile (an interesting man, who arguably did more than any other person to achieve the freedom of the press and had previously helped the abolitionist cause) wrote that he had 'no knowledge that Mr Wilberforce's humane advocacy for slaves was ever of that homely kind as to embrace the region of the home-cotton-slave-trade.'

He had a point. But, understandable though Carlile's concerns about factory conditions and the exploitation of the English working class might be, he then proceeded to use racist language to disparage all West Indians as lazy, and even to publish pro-slavery pamphlets!

The respectable abolitionists won; and 'wage-slavery' and child labour in British factories continued.

After the Reform Act of 1832 the new parliament passed the Slavery Abolition Act the very next year.

But British investment in slave-dependent industries contin-ued, especially the cotton industry which sourced its raw mate-rial from the southern states of the USA. Meanwhile the Empire started to pat itself on the back for having abolished slavery.

Abolition, rather than slavery itself, became the story, with Wilberforce as its saint and other key figures, especially black people, and the enslaved themselves, airbrushed out.

Has slavery been abolished?

Only slowly did abolition make its way round the world. It caused a civil war in the USA, echoes of which are still to be heard in Washington even now.

Mauritania was the last country to abolish, in 1981. However, it is thought that slavery still continues there in practice.

Does forced labour constitute slavery? Some human rights organisations have accused China of a form of 'modern slavery' in its 're-education camps' in Xinjiang, where it is said as many as a million Uyghurs, Kazakhs and others may be detained, and forced to work in cotton growing and manufacture, as well as producing solar panel materials. China denies this of course.

Charities have attempted to estimate the numbers of 'modern slaves', in today's world and the statistics, not to mention the definition, are open to question, but the total number might be as high as 40 million. And of those, perhaps 13,000 are in the UK. Whether the figures are accurate or not, there is surely reason to be concerned.

In Britain 'modern slavery' still exists in the form of human trafficking, sex exploitation, and domestic or agricultural forced labour. As an example, in 2018, 200 migrant workers were involved in flower picking near Helston in an incident investigated by the Gangmasters and Labour Abuse Authority.

Similar cases are known from East Anglia and Lincolnshire. When a crop has to be harvested quickly, a large number of workers are temporarily required, and gangmasters offer to provide them – and cheaply, probably not at the minimum wage. How easy is it for a farmer to check their credentials? And how strong is the incentive to accept the gang regardless, when a whole year's crop might otherwise be left to rot?

If I were CEO of a retailer of cheap clothing in the UK, would I dare to risk the future of my business and the jobs of my shop workers, let alone my family's livelihood, by looking too closely at my suppliers, when my competitors did not?

If history has a lesson for us, perhaps it is that when ethics and the economy don't agree, whether about slavery or climate change, it is very convenient for governments and businesses to shut their eyes to such things.

And also very easy for you and me not to notice.